WEEKLY WR READER®
EARLY LEARNING LIBRARY

Let's Read About Dinosaurs
Velociraptor

by Joanne Mattern
Illustrations by Jeffrey Magniat

Reading consultant: Susan Nations, M.Ed., author/literacy coach/
consultant in literacy development

Science consultant: Philip J. Currie, Ph.D., Professor and Canada Research
Chair of Dinosaur Palaeobiology at the University of Alberta, Canada

Please visit our web site at: www.garethstevens.com
For a free color catalog describing Weekly Reader® Early Learning Library's
list of high-quality books, call 1-877-445-5824 (USA) or 1-800-387-3178 (Canada).
Weekly Reader® Early Learning Library's fax: (414) 336-0164.

Library of Congress Cataloging-in-Publication Data

Mattern, Joanne, 1963-
    Velociraptor / by Joanne Mattern.
        p. cm. — (Let's read about dinosaurs)
    Includes bibliographical references and index.
    ISBN-13: 978-0-8368-7700-7 (lib. bdg.)
    ISBN-13: 978-0-8368-7707-6 (softcover)
    1. Velociraptor—Juvenile literature. I. Title.
    QE862.S3M332262   2007
    567.912—dc22   2006029992

This edition first published in 2007 by
Weekly Reader® Early Learning Library
A Member of the WRC Media Family of Companies
330 West Olive Street, Suite 100
Milwaukee, WI 53212 USA

Copyright © 2007 by Weekly Reader® Early Learning Library

Managing Editor: Valerie J. Weber
Art direction, cover and layout design: Tammy West

Printed in the United States of America

1 2 3 4 5 6 7 8 9 10 10 09 08 07 06

Note to Educators and Parents

Reading is such an exciting adventure for young children! They are beginning to integrate their oral language skills with written language. To encourage children along the path to early literacy, books must be colorful, engaging, and interesting; they should invite the young reader to explore both the print and the pictures.

Let's Read about Dinosaurs is a new series designed to help children read about some of their favorite — and most fearsome — animals. In each book, young readers will learn how each dinosaur survived so long ago.

Each book is specially designed to support the young reader in the reading process. The familiar topics are appealing to young children and invite them to read — and re-read — again and again. The full-color photographs and enhanced text further support the student during the reading process.

In addition to serving as wonderful picture books in schools, libraries, homes, and other places where children learn to love reading, these books are specifically intended to be read within an instructional guided reading group. This small group setting allows beginning readers to work with a fluent adult model as they make meaning from the text. After children develop fluency with the text and content, the book can be read independently. Children and adults alike will find these books supportive, engaging, and fun!

— Susan Nations, M.Ed., author, literacy coach, and consultant in literacy development

Velociraptor (vuh-LAH-suh-rap-tor) was small but fast and smart. It could hunt dinosaurs much bigger than itself!

5

Velociraptor stood as tall as a large dog. It only weighed about 33 pounds. That is as much as a three-year-old child!

7

Velociraptor ran on its two back legs. Only two of its toes touched the ground when it ran. Three large **claws** grew on its front arms.

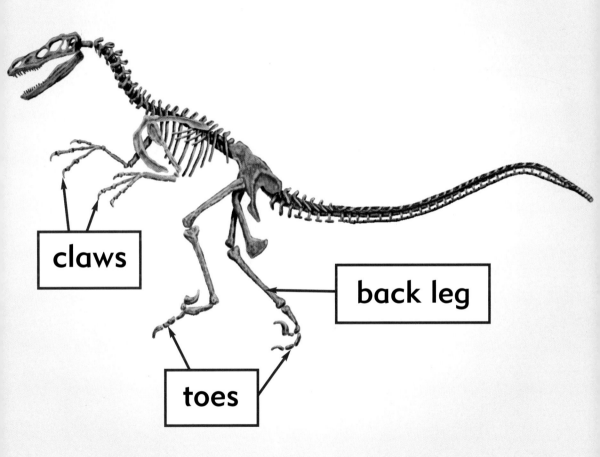

claws

back leg

toes

Velociraptor used these sharp claws to grab small dinosaurs and other animals.

Each foot had one claw that was bigger than the others. This curved claw could tear into Velociraptor's **prey**.

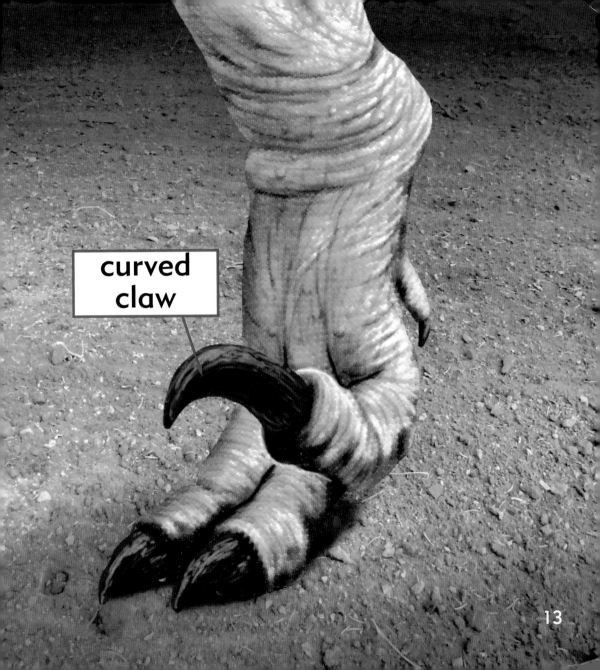

curved
claw

13

Velociraptor was smarter than most other dinosaurs. It hunted in groups to catch bigger dinosaurs. It often jumped on its prey's back.

Velociraptor's name means "speedy thief." This dinosaur also stole eggs from other dinosaurs to eat.

Velociraptor lived where it was hot and dry. Scientists think these dinosaurs traveled in groups.

Velociraptor died out long ago. No one knew about this dinosaur for many years. Then in 1923, a scientist found a Velociraptor **fossil**. Now we can see Velociraptor models in museums.

Glossary

fossil — bones or remains of animals and plants that lived a long time ago

models — copies of an animal, person, or object

museums — places where interesting objects are shown to the public

prey — animals that are hunted and eaten by other animals

scientists — people who study nature

speedy — fast

thief — someone who steals something

For More Information

Books

Swift Thief: The Adventure of Velociraptor. Dinosaur World (series). Michael Dahl (Picture Window Books)

Velociraptor. Carol Lindeen (Pebble Plus)

Velociraptor. Dinosaurs (series). Richard M. Gaines (Buddy Books)

Velociraptor. Gone Forever! (series). Rupert Matthews (Heinemann Library)

Web Site

A Velociraptor Named Bambi

www.wmnh.com/wmbam000.htm

This Web site has great photos of a Velociraptor skeleton found in Montana.

23

Index

arms 8

claws 8, 10, 12

eggs 16

feet 12

fossils 20

hunting 4, 14

legs 8

models 20

museums 20

prey 10, 12, 14

running 8

scientists 20

size 4, 6

toes 8

traveling 18

About the Author

Joanne Mattern has written more than 150 books for children. She has written about weird animals, sports, world cities, dinosaurs, and many other subjects. Joanne also works in her local library. She lives in New York State with her husband, three daughters, and assorted pets. She enjoys animals, music, going to baseball games, reading, and visiting schools to talk about her books.